THE
GOSPEL
PROJECT

GOD FIRST

His Law and His Love

J.D. Greear
& Trevin Wax

LifeWay Press®
Nashville, Tennessee

Item: 005606818
ISBN: 978-1-4300-2940-3
Dewey decimal classification number: 231.7
Subject heading: GOD \ TEN COMMANDMENTS \ SPIRITUAL LIFE

Eric Geiger
Vice President, Church Resources

Ed Stetzer
General Editor

Trevin Wax
Managing Editor

Faith Whatley
Director, Adult Ministry

Philip Nation
Director, Adult Ministry Publishing

Joel Polk
Content Editor

We believe that the Bible has God for its author; salvation for its end; and truth, without any mixture of error, for its matter and that all Scripture is totally true and trustworthy. To review LifeWay's doctrinal guideline, please visit *www.lifeway.com/doctrinalguideline*.

Unless otherwise noted, all Scripture quotations are taken from the Holman Christian Standard Bible®, copyright 1999, 2000, 2002, 2003, 2009 by Holman Bible Publishers. Used by permission.

For ordering or inquiries, visit *www.lifeway.com;* write LifeWay Small Groups; One LifeWay Plaza; Nashville, TN 37234-0152; or call toll free (800) 458-2772.

Printed in the United States of America.

Adult Ministry Publishing
LifeWay Church Resources
One LifeWay Plaza
Nashville, Tennessee 37234-0152

TABLE OF CONTENTS

ABOUT THE GOSPEL PROJECT

Some people see the Bible as a collection of stories with morals for life application. But it's so much more. Sure, the Bible has some stories in it, but it's also full of poetry, history, codes of law and civilization, songs, prophecy, letters—even a love letter. When you tie it all together, something remarkable happens. A story is revealed. One story. The story of redemption through Jesus. This is *The Gospel Project*.

When we begin to see the Bible as the story of redemption through Jesus Christ, God's plan to rescue the world from sin and death, our perspective changes. We no longer look primarily for what the Bible says about us but instead see what it tells us about God and what He has done. After all, it's the gospel that saves us, and when we encounter Jesus in the pages of Scripture, the gospel works on us, transforming us into His image. *We become God's gospel project.*

ABOUT THE WRITERS

Trevin Wax is managing editor for *The Gospel Project* and the author of *Clear Winter Nights*, *Gospel-Centered Teaching*, and *Counterfeit Gospels*. He has served in pastoral roles in churches in the United States and Romania. He and his wife, Corina, reside in Middle Tennessee with their three children.

J. D. Greear is the lead pastor of The Summit Church in Raleigh-Durham, North Carolina. He's the author of *Gospel: Recovering the Power That Made Christianity Revolutionary* and *Stop Asking Jesus into Your Heart*. He and his wife, Veronica, have four children.

Mike Cosper is the one of the founding pastors of Sojourn Community Church in Louisville, Kentucky, where he serves as the Executive Pastor of Worship and Arts. He's the author of *Rhythms of Grace: How the Church's Worship Tells the Story of the Gospel* and the co-author of *Faithmapping* with Daniel Montgomery. He and his wife, Sarah, have two daughters, Dorothy and Maggie. Mike wrote the second session in this study.

Barry Cram adapted this material for use with small groups.

HOW TO USE THIS STUDY

Welcome to *The Gospel Project*, a gospel-centered small-group study that dives deep into the things of God, lifts up Jesus, focuses on the grand story of Scripture, and drives participants to be on mission. This small-group Bible study provides opportunities to study the Bible and to encounter the living Christ. *The Gospel Project* provides you with tools and resources to purposefully study God's Word and to grow in the faith and knowledge of God's Son. And what's more, you can do so in the company of others, encouraging and building up one another. Here are some things to remember that will help you maximize the usefulness of this resource:

GATHER A GROUP. We grow in the faith best in community with other believers, as we love, encourage, correct, and challenge one another. The life of a disciple of Christ was never meant to be lived alone, in isolation.

PRAY. Pray regularly for your group members.

PREPARE. This resource includes the Bible study content, three devotionals, and discussion questions for each session. Work through the session and devotionals in preparation for each group session. Take notes and record your own questions. Also consider the follow-up questions so you are ready to participate in and add to the discussion, bringing up your own notes and questions where appropriate.

RESOURCE YOURSELF. Make good use of the additional resources available on the Web at *www.gospelproject.com/additionalresources* and search for this specific title. Download a podcast. Read a blog post. Be intentional about learning from others in the faith.

GROUP TIME. Gather together with your group to discuss the session and devotional content. Work through the follow-up questions and your own questions. Discuss the material and the implications for the lives of believers and the mission to which we have been called.

OVERFLOW. Remember …*The Gospel Project* is not just a Bible study. *We* are the project. The gospel is working on us. Don't let your preparation time be simply about the content. Let the truths of God's Word soak in as you study. Let God work on your heart first, and then pray that He will change the hearts of the other people in your group.

THE
GOSPEL PROJECT

Session 1

God First in Love and Pursuit

INDIVIDUAL STUDY

The Ten Commandments have made the news in recent years. No, they've never been debated in Congress, but they have been carved out on the walls throughout the courtrooms across North America. Some have protested their presence, and others have defended their history and precedent. In some instances, the Commandments have been removed. Other cities have permitted them to remain because they are commonly accepted as a cultural artifact.

> Do you see the Ten Commandments as an example of a universal moral code? Or do you see them as specific revelation of God to His people? Explain.

> In what ways do you see the Ten Commandments revealing the heart of God to and for His people?

Studying the Ten Commandments makes us wonder about the laws that surround them. What is the point of obscure Old Testament laws about clothing, food, purity, and cleanliness? If we're not keeping every single law we find in the Old Testament, why should we keep the Ten Commandments? Do we pick and choose which laws are still relevant? And why do we need laws in the first place? Didn't Jesus fulfill all that stuff in the Old Testament?

In this session, we set the framework for understanding the purpose behind the Ten Commandments by looking at the law of God in general. The law is more than just a stone monument. Acting in love, God pursued them first with His law. In the Scriptures, we will see that the law of God is an expression of the love of God.

Over the next week engage the daily study sections associated with *God First* as a way to better understand the law of God as an act of love. There are three daily readings to prepare you before the group meets for this session. Interact with the Scriptures, and be ready to interact with your small group.

1 The Beginning of the Law is Love

Before we look at each Commandment, it's helpful to get a feel for the purpose for the law altogether. Why all these rules and regulations? What does God want from us? And what's His motivation for giving us the law? Take a look at Moses' words in Deuteronomy 10:

> ¹² And now, Israel, what does the LORD your God ask of you except to fear the LORD your God by walking in all His ways, to love Him, and to worship the LORD your God with all your heart and all your soul? ¹³ Keep the LORD's commands and statutes I am giving you today, for your own good. ¹⁴ The heavens, indeed the highest heavens, belong to the LORD your God, as does the earth and everything in it. ¹⁵ Yet the LORD was devoted to your fathers and loved them. He chose their descendants after them—He chose you out of all the peoples, as it is today. ¹⁶ Therefore, circumcise your hearts and don't be stiff-necked any longer. ¹⁷ For the LORD your God is the God of gods and Lord of lords, the great, mighty, and awesome God, showing no partiality and taking no bribe. ¹⁸ He executes justice for the fatherless and the widow, and loves the foreigner, giving him food and clothing. ¹⁹ You also must love the foreigner, since you were foreigners in the land of Egypt. ²⁰ You are to fear Yahweh your God and worship Him. Remain faithful to Him and take oaths in His name. ²¹ He is your praise and He is your God, who has done for you these great and awesome works your eyes have seen. ²² Your fathers went down to Egypt, 70 people in all, and now the LORD your God has made you as numerous as the stars of the sky.
>
> DEUTERONOMY 10:12-22

We won't understand the purpose behind the law of God until we see how it connects to love. And love is at the heart of God's law.

In your own words, restate Moses' explanation for the law when he told the people to obey the Lord's commands and statutes.

Did you ever hear your mom say, "Eat your vegetables. It's for your own good"? This is God saying the same thing. He loved them. He chose to rescue them! According to Moses, God's love for His people is the foundation of His merciful rescue of the children of Israel from the hand of slavery. The Ten Commandments aren't given as a way to work for salvation from

God; they're given after God has already worked salvation for us. They're not given so we can rescue ourselves; they're given to those God has rescued.

> What are the dangers of focusing on God's law apart from His love?
> What role does God's rescue play in our ability to live according to His commands?

The law of God goes beyond His actions for us. It shows us how we are to live in light of God's character. The focus turns to God's love for the foreigner, the fatherless, and the widow. Love for God is expressed in how we treat others. It's allowing God to use us to love others who are in the state we once were—praying they'll be brought to salvation, too.

The beginning of God's law is love, but it doesn't always seem to be our reality. Some people love the structure that comes from rules. So they focus on the rules and conform. Some people see rules inhibiting life and restricting their personality. So live their lives spontaneously and throw the rules out the window. Scripture doesn't line up with either side. Those who love rules will find that Scripture consistently directs our attention back to the point of the rules. The law itself is not the point but the loving purpose flowing from God's heart.

> Which kind of person are you—one who stresses outward conformity to God's law or one who values spontaneity and authenticity? What are the dangers of both extremes?

> What are some aspects of Christian morality that people in our culture believe are joy-suppressing rather than joy-enhancing? How should Christians respond to this view of God's law?

2 The Demand of the Law is Perfection

Therefore, love the LORD your God and always keep His
mandate and His statutes, ordinances, and commands.
DEUTERONOMY 11:1

Two words in this verse may strike fear into your heart. The first is "*love* the LORD your God." We know from Jesus' words that obedience is the sign of love. In other words, the way we express our love for God is to obey Him without a bad attitude. We are to do the right thing for the right reason with the right attitude. And that leads us to the other scary word, "always." We are to "*always* keep His mandate and statutes, ordinances, and commands." God demands total obedience from a loving heart.

> **What is your reaction to the command to obey in Deuteronomy 11:1? Does it make you want to be more disciplined or make you despair? Why?**

One of the things the law shows us is God's absolute, stunning holiness. There is no trace of sin or evil in Him. There is no stain of rebellion or wrongdoing. He is holy love.

Because the law of God accurately reflects His holiness, it's no wonder that the law of God immediately shows us our sinfulness. Have you ever cleaned up a classroom or conference room full of old carpet? Everything looks clean when you finish. But once the desks and chairs are moved out of the way and the sun shines through the window at a different angle, the floor looks horrible. The darkness has a way of making a dirty floor look clean. But sunlight has a way of exposing a dirty, stained floor for what it really is.

The law of God is like that. It's brilliant in its beauty, and we are thankful for what it reveals about God. And yet it quickly shows us how we don't measure up. We understand our sin in light of His holiness. It's easy to see any kind of sin in our hearts when the light of His law shines down. The demand of the Commandments is absolutely and totally perfect. That kind of reality would drive any self-aware man to their knees.

> **Describe the kind of parents that demand perfection from their children. How does that description line with how you view God?**

That's where Jesus comes in. He met the demand of the law. He lived the perfect life we could not live, upheld the law at every point we failed, and loved God and others the way humans were always intended to. Take the two scary words we talked about earlier: love and always. Now, apply them to Jesus. Think about it. He loved God always. That's why He was the perfect substitute for us on the cross.

> Why do you think we have a difficult time putting into practice all that Christ commands? What gets in the way for you?

> How does understanding the demands of the law help increase our desire and gratitude for grace?

3 The End of the Law is Love

We've seen that the demand of the law is perfection—God expects absolute and total obedience, which He then offers through the person and work of His Son, Jesus Christ. Now, we might be tempted to let our gratitude for Christ's work on our behalf lead us to passivity, as if the law no longer has anything to say to us. If Jesus fulfilled the law, then what's left for us?

According to the New Testament, we are not under the Law of Moses but the law of love as expressed by Jesus Christ. Because of the Spirit's presence in our hearts, we are empowered to obey. What does this obedience look like? Look at Romans 13.

> [8] Do not owe anyone anything, except to love one another, for the one who loves another has fulfilled the law. [9] The commandments:
> Do not commit adultery;
> do not murder;
> do not steal;
> do not covet;
> and whatever other commandment—all are summed
> up by this: Love your neighbor as yourself.
> [10] Love does no wrong to a neighbor. Love, therefore, is the fulfillment of the law.
> [11] Besides this, knowing the time, it is already the hour for you to wake up
> from sleep, for now our salvation is nearer than when we first believed.
> [12] The night is nearly over, and the daylight is near, so let us discard
> the deeds of darkness and put on the armor of light. [13] Let us walk with
> decency, as in the daylight: not in carousing and drunkenness; not in sexual
> impurity and promiscuity; not in quarreling and jealousy. [14] But put on the
> Lord Jesus Christ, and make no plans to satisfy the fleshly desires.
> ROMANS 13:8-14

If the end of the law is love, then what about all the other laws in the Old Testament? Paul didn't refer to the laws about ceremonial observance or civil disputes in this passage. He referred back to the Commandments about loving our neighbors.

As Christians, we believe Jesus fulfilled all of the law in our place, and yet we recognize there are different kinds of laws in the Old Testament. For centuries, Christians have divided the laws of Israel into three categories: civil laws (theocratic government), ceremonial laws (sacrificial system), and moral laws (the Ten Commandments). We believe the Ten Commandments are moral laws that transcend time and culture.

We are not bound to keep the civil laws that governed the life of Israel since we're no longer in a theocracy. We're not bound to keep the ceremonial laws because they pointed to Christ and have been fulfilled. We do live according to the moral laws, though, not because they were unfulfilled by Christ. We live by them because they are rooted in God's character and are the expression of our love for our neighbor. The end of the law is love. And love leads us back to laws that help us uphold our love for others as an expression of our love for God.

What is the relationship between our love for God and our love for others? How does love for our neighbor impact our motivation for evangelism and service?

One of the main reasons we are to live holy lives today is because we live in light of salvation. We are God's people! Since the resurrection of Jesus, the new day has dawned. If we continue to live in disobedience and sin, we are refusing to live in the light. We are closing the shades around the window, keeping out the sunlight that comes from Christ's finished work for us. Paul's Letter to the Romans urges us to fulfill the law by living in the light of its love.

What does continual breaking of God's law say about our belief in Christ?

How does understanding that the day of salvation is drawing near give a sense of urgency to our evangelism?

GROUP STUDY

Warm Up

Atheist and comedian George Carlin once said:

> The real reason that we can't have the Ten Commandments
> in a courthouse: You cannot post 'Thou shalt not
> steal,' 'Thou shalt not commit adultery,' and 'Thou
> shalt not lie' in a building full of lawyers, judges, and
> politicians. It creates a hostile work environment.[2]

We bring attention to George Carlin's comment not because we agree with him, but because many people share his view on God, religion, and the Ten Commandments. Simply, they reject it.

> How do you respond to someone who objects to the Ten
> Commandments by saying they are out-of-date and no longer relevant
> for us today?

Because we see the Ten Commandments on display in public places, we start to think of them as "stand alone" Commandments—like a portion of the Bible that's isolated from the rest of the story line. Instead, we ought to see the Commandments within their context of the Old Testament law. And we should see the law within the context of God's love for His people. Maybe that's why the opposition is so stern from those who truly reject them. They don't see the Ten Commandments as "stand alone" laws.

> If you accept the Ten Commandments (with the Bible and God) as "all
> or nothing," what do you think is the most offensive commandment to
> those who refuse to believe in God? Why?

> Can you explain why it's important to understand the context for the Ten
> Commandments? In your own words, give it a try.

Discussion

Understanding the love of God behind the law of God is crucial in seeing the gospel story that is embedded deep within the story of Israel. God has never once lowered the bar for holiness and perfection. The law would reveal that! Instead God found a way to bring us up to meet this perfect standard when He brought Jesus back to life again.

During this time you'll have an opportunity to discuss what God revealed to you during the week. Listed below are some of the questions from your daily reading assignments. They will guide your small-group discussion.

1. How did you restate Moses' explanation for the law when he told the people to obey the Lord's commands and statutes (see Deut. 10:12-22)?

2. What are the dangers of focusing on God's law apart from His love? What role does God's rescue play in our ability to live according to His commands?

3. What are some aspects of Christian morality that people in our culture believe are joy-suppressing rather than joy-enhancing? How should Christians respond to this view of God's law?

4. What is your initial reaction to the command to obey in Deuteronomy 11:1? Does it make you want to be more disciplined or make you despair? Why?

5. Describe the kind of parents that demand perfection from their children. How does that description line with how you view God?

6. Why do you think we have a difficult time putting into practice all that Christ commands? What gets in the way for you? How does understanding the demands of the law help increase our desire and gratitude for grace?

7. What is the relationship between our love for God and our love for others? How does love for our neighbor impact our motivation for evangelism and service?

Conclusion

God's law is given to us because He loves us. He pursues us. From beginning to end, we see the law as an expression of God's love for His people. Pastor Randall Grossman sees the purpose of the law as a map, a muzzle, and a mirror. It's a map because it guides our behavior and shows us how to live in light of God's salvation and for His glory. It's a muzzle because it restrains evil and bad behavior in society. And it's a mirror because it reflects us and shows us our sin, leading us to recognize our need for our Savior.[3]

As we examine each of the Ten Commandments, as well as the purpose of God's law in general, we'll see how this law guides our conduct, restrains us from sin, and points us to Jesus. So let's look at the Ten Commandments with new eyes—not as a cultural artifact that belongs on stone monument outside of courthouses but as an expression of God's love and mercy inscribed on our hearts.

Spend some time praying this for you and for your group:

> "God, I need Your guidance and the Holy Spirit's conviction as I begin this journey through Your Word. Help me see the law as relevant for my life today."

1. Ronald Reagan, as quoted in Ross English, *The United States Congress* (New York City: Manchester University Press, 2003), 161.
2. George Carlin, *Complaints and Grievances*, DVD, directed by Rocco Urbisci (New York City: HBO, 2001).
3. Randall Grossman, as quoted in Philip Ryken, *Written in Stone* (Wheaton: Crossway, 2003), 27.
4. Charles Spurgeon, *The Parables of Our Lord*, vol. 3 in *Miracles and Parables of Our Lord* (Grand Rapids: Baker, reprinted 1989), 413.

As the sharp needle prepares the way for the thread, so the piercing law makes a way for the bright silver thread of divine grace.[4]

CHARLES SPURGEON

NOTES

THE GOSPEL PROJECT

Session 2

God First in Religious Intent

Well-intentioned Christ-followers like you and me can unintentionally sabotage the work of the Lord we claim to serve when we become so focused on what we see as the agenda of God that we lose touch with the heart of God.

LARRY OSBORNE

INDIVIDUAL STUDY

Did you know that in Massachusetts it's illegal to drive with a gorilla in your backseat? In California you can't eat oranges while sitting in a bathtub. In Georgia it's against the law to walk around with an ice cream cone in your back pocket.

As absurd as these laws may seem, there was once a time when a social challenge motivated lawmakers to address these issues. The ice cream cone law, for instance, was enacted to prevent people from stealing horses. A thief would stick an ice cream cone in his back pocket, and the horse, lured by the treat, would follow him home. The thief could say he never touched the horse!

Laws taken out of context or removed from the story of the community that enacted them sound absurd. But laws exist to guide and protect us. The story of a community is the key to understanding the community's laws. This is as true with odd laws in contemporary society as it is with the Bible. The law—the commands we find in the Old Testament—is something we have to understand in the context of the story of God's people. Unfortunately, many of us view biblical laws with the same sense of bewilderment that we have for contemporary laws about gorillas and ice cream cones.

The Old Testament makes our heads spin with all of its laws. Cynics and skeptics will cite these laws as evidence of Christianity's superstition, and in response, many Christians dismiss the law as something erased by the gospel. Jesus encountered these attitudes in His ministry. His life was a rebuke to both those who dismissed the law altogether and to those who used the law as a prop for their own religious egos. Just as some see the law as silly and antiquated, others see it as a path to justify themselves. They think that by obeying the rules—whether religious rules of the Bible or some unwritten social code of what "good people" do—they prove themselves worthy to God.

How would you describe your general attitude toward the law in Scripture?

What are some unwritten "laws" Christians use to measure one another?

This week engage the daily study sections on your own. Each of them centers on a different aspect of Jesus and the law. There are three daily readings to prepare you before the group meets for this session. Interact with the Scriptures, and be ready to interact with your small group.

1 Jesus Upheld the Law

In the Sermon on the Mount, Jesus confronted misconceptions about the law. Take a look at what He said:

> [17] "Don't assume that I came to destroy the Law or the Prophets. I did not come to destroy but to fulfill. [18] For I assure you: Until heaven and earth pass away, not the smallest letter or one stroke of a letter will pass from the law until all things are accomplished. [19] Therefore, whoever breaks one of the least of these commands and teaches people to do so will be called least in the kingdom of heaven. But whoever practices and teaches these commands will be called great in the kingdom of heaven. [20] For I tell you, unless your righteousness surpasses that of the scribes and Pharisees, you will never enter the kingdom of heaven.
>
> MATTHEW 5:17-20

Here Jesus gives a new way to see the law. He came to fulfill the law (v. 17). And yet He urged His followers to practice and teach the law (v. 19) with a righteousness that exceeds that of the scribes and Pharisees (v. 20), who were the most respectable law-abiders of His day. So what did Jesus mean?

First, we can see that Jesus upheld the Law: "Don't assume that I came to destroy the Law or the Prophets," He said. Let's put this comment in context. Matthew 5 opens the Sermon on the Mount, where Jesus shattered the assumptions of His audience about who is blessed, who is righteous, and what God expects from His people. Verses 3-12 are called "the Beatitudes." Here Jesus declared that the poor, the needy, the meek, the persecuted, the peacemakers, and the suffering are the ones who are blessed. It's a stunning reversal of the way people tend to see the world.

Most of us carry an implicit understanding that says, "If we do good things, good things happen to us." That understanding gets baptized in all kinds of religious ways. We go from "If we do good things, good things happen" to "If we do good things, God owes us a blessing." It might be health or wealth or just plain happiness, but we tend to think that we can earn or deserve God's favor because of our religious obedience.

> How do you see the attitude that we can earn God's favor through our obedience at work in your life?

The Beatitudes put an end to the idea of earning God's favor. Jesus said God blesses those who are broken and downtrodden, those who recognize their need. The rest of Jesus' sermon disrupts all kinds of ideas about religion, law, and obedience. Jesus connected murder back to hatred and adultery to lust. We can't skate past the Ten Commandments and congratulate ourselves for not killing someone or cheating on our spouse. Even our daydreams condemn us.

Rightly understood, we can see Jesus' life and teaching as perfectly obedient to the law (see Heb. 4:15). His life and teaching is also the law's fullest and clearest revelation. These inversions and reversals don't mean Jesus was throwing out the law. On the contrary, it's fair to say that no one in history has cared more about the law than Jesus. Why? Because the law is actually about Him! (See John 5:39,46.)

The good news is that Jesus fulfills the law. Paul would later write that Jesus is the "end of the law for righteousness to everyone who believes" (Rom. 10:4). The law comes at us like a blaring announcement, declaring to any who hear it that we have fallen short; we have no hope of living up to God's glorious standard (see Rom. 3:23).

But Jesus stands between us and that declaration. In fact, He ends the accusations entirely, having perfectly kept the law in our place.

> What is the difference between Jesus abolishing the law and Jesus fulfilling the law? Why is it important to remember that Jesus upheld the law?

> What are some habits God wants His people to cultivate so that obedience becomes second nature?

> How can we keep these habits from becoming legalistic burdens or heartless routines?

2 Religion Disguised as Disobedience

Timothy Keller said, "'Religion,' or moralism, is avoiding God as Lord and Savior by developing a moral righteousness and then presenting it to God in an effort to show that he 'owes' you. The gospel, however, has nothing to do with our developing a righteousness we give God so He owes us; it is God's developing and giving us righteousness through Jesus Christ."[2]

[1] Then Pharisees and scribes came from Jerusalem to Jesus
and asked, [2] "Why do Your disciples break the tradition of the
elders? For they don't wash their hands when they eat!"
[3] He answered them, "And why do you break God's
commandment because of your tradition? [4] For God said:
Honor your father and your mother; and,
The one who speaks evil of father or mother must be put to death.
[5] But you say, 'Whoever tells his father or mother, "Whatever
benefit you might have received from me is a gift committed to
the temple"— [6] he does not have to honor his father.' In this way,
you have revoked God's word because of your tradition.
MATTHEW 15:1-6

Before we begin, we need to define a couple of terms. The word *religion* can simply mean a way of practicing spirituality, and in this sense, it's a good word. James used the word with a positive connotation when he wrote.

"Pure and undefiled religion before our God and Father is this: to look after orphans and widows in their distress and to keep oneself unstained by the world" (Jas. 1:27). By this, James meant that caring for orphans and widows is an authentic kind of spirituality and religion, a practice consistent with the heart of God.

But more often, the word *religion* has a negative connotation. Here we will use it in reference to efforts to earn God's approval. We do things religiously as an attempt to cleanse ourselves from sin and make ourselves acceptable to God—a task the gospel shows to be futile apart from Jesus.

How have you defined religion in the past? In what ways has keeping religious kept you away from God?

In this way, the scribes and Pharisees were professional religious people whose lives were devoted to teaching and obeying practices that made one clean or unclean, acceptable or unacceptable to God. They were experts on both the law of God and the religious traditions of Israel, many of which were treated with authority equal to the Scriptures.

Their religious obedience was compliant but disingenuous. It was inauthentic paying fierce attention to the letter of the law while missing its spirit entirely. The Pharisees were wearing a mask that made them look holy, but inside they were rotten.

Which brings us to the second term that needs definition—*hypocrite*. The word itself refers to an actor who wears a mask to play a role. Jesus saw their righteousness as an act, a show they were putting on, a mere mask that hid something insidious. His anger flowed freely here because their hypocrisy had terrible, flesh-and-blood consequences.

> **Do you agree or disagree with this statement—"Humans are naturally religious" (referring to earning God's approval or proving ourselves worthy)? Why or why not?**

Look at the Pharisees' attack on Jesus. They criticized Him because His disciples didn't follow the traditions of the elders regarding hand-washing before meals. This tradition wasn't biblical. But keeping this tradition actually kept them from obeying God. No wonder Jesus was angry! The religious elite were neglecting God's commandment so they could keep more money. They touted their own obedience and nitpicked the obedience of others, blind to the way their traditions trampled the Word of God (and frankly, the order of creation—God's Commandment that families would honor parents and care for one another).

> **How does a focus on external behavior lead to judgmental attitudes?**

> **What are some traditions we practice that might keep us from full, heart-level obedience to God?**

3 Connecting Our Heart to Our Behavior

¹⁰ Summoning the crowd, He told them, "Listen and understand:
¹¹ It's not what goes into the mouth that defiles a man, but
what comes out of the mouth, this defiles a man."
¹² Then the disciples came up and told Him, "Do You know that
the Pharisees took offense when they heard this statement?"
¹³ He replied, "Every plant that My heavenly Father didn't plant
will be uprooted. ¹⁴ Leave them alone! They are blind guides.
And if the blind guide the blind, both will fall into a pit."
¹⁵ Then Peter replied to Him, "Explain this parable to us."
¹⁶ "Are even you still lacking in understanding?" He asked. ¹⁷ "Don't you realize
that whatever goes into the mouth passes into the stomach and is eliminated?
¹⁸ But what comes out of the mouth comes from the heart, and this defiles
a man. ¹⁹ For from the heart come evil thoughts, murders, adulteries, sexual
immoralities, thefts, false testimonies, blasphemies. ²⁰ These are the things
that defile a man, but eating with unwashed hands does not defile a man."
MATTHEW 15:10-20

You can summarize this teaching with five words: It's all about the heart. The crowd was so concerned with externals—what they ate, how they cleaned themselves, whom they were with, and how they distinguished themselves from others. But Jesus said, "It's the heart. It's the heart. It's the heart."

Shortly before this incident, Jesus made the connection between words and the heart: "For the mouth speaks from the overflow of the heart" (Matt. 12:34). Here He built on that connection, showing how our words reveal the corruption that's within. The crowd must have been stunned by this statement. They had lived their whole lives according to careful dietary rules and restraints in order to remain ceremonially clean. "It's the heart," Jesus said, shaking up the orderly world they understood.

How does God judge in ways different from us? What are some examples in Scripture that illustrate these differences?

When Jesus' disciples wanted Him to know He'd offended the Pharisees, Jesus was unrelenting. The Pharisees didn't just offend His holy righteousness; they were doing immeasurable harm. Jesus warned that they would eventually be uprooted by God. He dismissed their importance by saying, "Leave them alone! They are blind guides. And if the blind guide the blind, both will fall into a pit."

The people of Israel—the Pharisees in particular—saw themselves as guides of the blind. They believed that since God had given them the law, they were suited to be guides for the rest of the world. But Jesus knew that this was a case of the blind leading the blind. Elsewhere He told them, "You pore over the Scriptures because you think you have eternal life in them, yet they testify about Me" (John 5:39). The people's inability to see Jesus made them dangerous guides for a blind world.

The disciples found themselves as confused as ever, and Jesus gave one more explanation to them. Jesus taught them a fascinating truth. Sins like murder, adultery, sexual immorality, theft, false testimonies, and blasphemies—all of which are external and public actions—Jesus claimed these sins come from the heart! In other words, Jesus was telling them—and us—that we're far worse off than we ever thought. The religious leaders' obsession with ritualistic hand-washing and food laws offered them no real protection from our sin or real unrighteousness.

> How should the truth that sin has penetrated to our very core change the way we think and feel about the law? How does it change the way we feel about our responsibilities toward God and others?

> What is the role of the heart in our part of God's mission? Why is it important that our heart be aligned with God's heart for the lost?

It's that indwelling power of sin that ultimately leads us into all kinds of trouble. All of our sin has its roots in the heart, and Jesus' harsh words are the rebuke of One who loves us. It's the frustration of a Teacher who wants His disciples to understand that there's only one effective cure for all that ails human nature—and that's Him. It does us no good to focus on obeying God if it doesn't come from a renewed heart.

GROUP STUDY

Warm Up

Even though some Christians tend to disregard the Old Testament as irrelevant to our faith today, Jesus declared God's law to be authoritative and necessary for us. The law is like a teacher who shows us God's holiness, our sinfulness, and our need for salvation. In fulfilling the law through His life, death, and resurrection, Jesus enables us to attain a righteousness that is greater than the Pharisees.

The apostle Paul, an ex-Pharisee himself, changed his mind completely about law-keeping and righteousness. He learned to value something much more that religious obedience.

Read Philippians 3:7-11:

> [7] But whatever were gains to me I now consider loss for the sake of Christ.
> [8] What is more, I consider everything a loss because of the surpassing worth of knowing Christ Jesus my Lord, for whose sake I have lost all things.
> I consider them garbage, that I may gain Christ [9] and be found in him, not having a righteousness of my own that comes from the law, but that which is through faith in Christ—the righteousness that comes from God on the basis of faith. [10] I want to know Christ—yes, to know the power of his resurrection and participation in his sufferings, becoming like him in his death, [11] and so, somehow, attaining to the resurrection from the dead.

What is the difference between a righteousness "of my own from the law" and a righteousness that is "through faith in Christ" (Phil. 3:9)?

Why is it important to rely on Christ and not our own righteousness?

Describe how healthy religion can lead people to the heart of God.

Discussion

Jesus demanded obedience from His followers, but His idea of obedience went beyond willpower. Religious activity can become a way of hiding our rebellious hearts and focusing all our attention on the things we do instead of who we are. In exposing the Pharisees' obsession with outward rituals, Jesus showed the connection between the heart and our behavior. Only the gospel changes the heart, and therefore, only the gospel can lead to lasting change in our lives.

During this time you will have an opportunity to discuss what God revealed to you during the week. Listed below are some of the questions from your daily reading assignments. They will guide your small-group discussion

1. Why do you think it is important to remember that Jesus upheld the law? What is the difference between Jesus abolishing the law and Jesus fulfilling the law?

2. In what ways do you see the law being an expression of God's grace?

3. What are some habits God wants His people to cultivate so that obedience becomes second nature? How can we keep these habits from becoming legalistic burdens or heartless routines?

4. How have you defined religion in the past? In what ways has keeping religious kept you away from God?

5. How does a focus on external behavior lead to judgmental attitudes? What are some traditions we practice that might keep us from full, heart-level obedience to God?

6. What is the role of the heart in our part of God's mission? Why is it important that our heart be aligned with God's heart for the lost?

7. What are some areas where the law shows our disobedience? How does the gospel address the primacy of the heart?

Conclusion

There are so many ways to make someone obey God. You can make them fearful of the consequences if they don't obey. You can give them an incentive and offer a reward. Some people obey because they are competitive and have something to prove. But none of these reasons actually gets to the heart of God.

Keeping God at the center of any religious activity requires a renewed heart. The gospel is a vibrant alternative to finding hope in obedience and rule-checking. It starts with the heart. Rather than trying to patch up the broken and empty things we carry within us, Jesus chucks out the old heart and gives us something brand new. The new heart becomes a meeting place for us and God. It's a place where we can transform our minds and keep God first. Then and only then can the good things that we do flow authentically from who we are.

Spend some time praying this for you and for your group:

O Lord, you have mercy on all; take away from me my sins, and mercifully set me ablaze with the fire of your Holy Spirit. Take away from me the heart of stone, and give me a human heart, a heart to love and adore you, a heart to delight in you, to follow and enjoy you, for Christ's sake. Amen.[3]
ST. JEROME

1. Larry Osborne, *Accidental Pharisees* (Grand Rapids: Zondervan, 2012), 194
2. Timothy Keller, *Center Church* (Grand Rapids: Zondervan, 2012), 63.
3. Jerome, as quoted in Thomas C. Oden and Joel E. Elowsky, ed., *On the Way to the Cross: 40 Days with the Church Fathers* (Downers Grove: InterVarsity Press, 2011), 76.
4. Warren Wiersbe, *The Bible Exposition Commentary*, vol. 2 (Colorado Springs: Cook Communications, 2001), 212.

Law and Gospel go together, for the Law without the Gospel is diagnosis without remedy; but the Gospel without Law is only the Good News of salvation for people who don't believe they need it because they have never heard the bad news of judgment. The Law is not the Gospel, but the Gospel is not lawless.[4]

WARREN WIERSBE

NOTES

THE GOSPEL PROJECT

Session 3

God First in All of Life

The First Commandment reminds us to keep the main thing the main thing. ... Everything begins and ends with God. He always comes first.[1]

WINFIELD BEVINS

INDIVIDUAL STUDY

The Ten Commandments that sum up the Old Testament law begin with a Commandment that sums up the other nine. Think about it. Breaking the First Commandment is what inevitably leads us to breaking the others. When our hearts turn away from God, we crave other things to take His place, which leads us to act in ways that are contrary to His good design for our lives. In fact, we could say that breaking the other Commandments is the expression of breaking the First—putting other gods before the one true God. It's the inevitable domino-effect that unravels our would-be life of obedient worship.

God gave us this Commandment first for a reason. It affects every attitude, ambition, and action we have in all of life. It paves the way for worship—the everyday-Romans-12, living-sacrifice, lifestyle kind of worship. And since all of humanity has been created to worship God, this Commandment serves as a preeminent and constant reminder of who deserves our worship. We can't escape this aspect of who we are! We are all worshipers. Even the non-religious worship something. It's like breathing. It's a part of the human experience. The question isn't if we worship something. The question is what is the object of our worship?

> How does abandoning the First Commandment give the Enemy permission to unravel your life and skew your view of God?

> In what ways does all of this wreck your life of worship?

God has demonstrated His love by redeeming us. As an affectionate Father, He desires and deserves to have first place in our lives. The only way we can obey this command is to have a life-transforming encounter with the true God who has given His Son for our redemption and His Spirit for our mission. In this session about the First Commandment, we set the stage for this conversation: that we should desire what God truly deserves—to be first in all of life.

Over the next week engage these daily study sections. Center your mind's attention and heart's affection on this notion: that God's place in your life should be first place in your life. Interact with the Scriptures, and be ready to interact with your small group.

God Shows His Love by Redeeming Us

> [1] Moses summoned all Israel and said to them, "Israel, listen to the statutes and ordinances I am proclaiming as you hear them today. Learn and follow them carefully. [2] The LORD our God made a covenant with us at Horeb. [3] He did not make this covenant with our fathers, but with all of us who are alive here today. [4] The LORD spoke to you face to face from the fire on the mountain. [5] At that time I was standing between the LORD and you to report the word of the LORD to you, because you were afraid of the fire and did not go up the mountain. And He said: [6] I am the LORD your God, who brought you out of the land of Egypt, out of the place of slavery.
>
> **DEUTERONOMY 5:1-6**

Let's note three things in this passage. Do you see the emphasis on God's relationship with His people? The passage begins with Moses reminding the people that God made a covenant with them (see vv. 2-3). This is a God who makes personal promises. He's not a distant deity hurling thunderbolts from afar. He's a God of holy and righteous love who wants the best for the people He has created and redeemed.

Notice the emphasis on God's grace in revealing Himself to the people of Israel (see vv. 4-5). God was under no obligation to give the law to His people. He could have left them to figure out the best way to live on their own. But in love, God revealed Himself and His character. He allowed Moses to be a *mediator* for the people. This desire for a mediator—someone to plead to God on our behalf—is important for understanding how the Old Testament paves the way for Jesus, the only Mediator between God and man (see 1 Tim. 2:5-6).

Finally, note how God has worked on behalf of His people (see Deut. 5:6). This isn't a God who makes promises with words only; He does what He says. God said He's the Lord God who brought His people out of slavery in Egypt. He's the glorious God who has done great things. And these great things are on behalf of His beloved people. So God works for the good of His people and for the glory of His name.

What does the First Commandment require? What does the First Commandment forbid?

Think about how God's law and God's love work together for the good of His people. How have you experienced this in your own life?

How does our view of commands or rules change when they are separated from personal relationship?

2 God Deserves First Place in Our Lives

The covenant relationship has been established. It serves as the foundation for God's law. Here is the First Commandment.

> Do not have other gods besides Me.
> **DEUTERONOMY 5:7**

Sounds simple enough, right? The Hebrew word there for *besides Me* could be rendered *in My presence*. Don't have any other gods in My presence. Nothing else can qualify as a god in your life. The true God is to be number One.

In our day, we don't like narrow, exclusive options. We might think God is constraining and restricting our choices. But isn't this how love is expressed? Imagine if a husband were to tell his wife, "Honey, you're number one. No matter how many other wives I take, you'll be my first." Yes, that makes for compelling reality television. No, that doesn't make for a good marriage. Love demands exclusivity. A wife doesn't want to be number one. She wants to be the only one! Her love for her husband would accept nothing less. This isn't a demand based on exclusivity. This is a based on love.

So, love and exclusivity aren't at odds with each other. God's demand for loyalty is His display of love.

Why is it appropriate for God to demand first place in our lives?

You may think that you've got this First Commandment covered. You may think to yourself, "I don't call anything or anyone else 'God' in my life. I don't bow down to or worship anything or anyone else. I don't pray to anything or anyone else. And I sure don't have any little statues or shrines in my house. Let's move on." But here's where we need to explore more deeply the meaning of putting other things or people before God.

This is where we come to a key biblical concept—*idolatry*.

What is an idol? It's anything or anyone we put in the place of God in our lives. An idol is anything we consider so central, fundamental, or essential to our life that we couldn't imagine life without it. An idol is anyone we love, trust, and/or obey more than God. And the reason breaking the First Commandment leads to breaking the others is that idolatry is the gateway to all other sins. If we look deeply into the ways we disobey God, we'll usually find idolatry at the root.

Think about it like this. The areas in our lives where we are breaking the Commandments are like smoke from a fire. Don't focus on the smoke. That's just the effect or symptom of the fire. Instead, follow the trail of smoke back to the source. The fire you find are at the altars of the idols you are worshiping. Sin management (aka, changing our behavior) isn't the answer. We don't fix heart issues with obedience. We must go back to the attitude that leads to the action—the idolatrous heart. Replacing God with something (or someone) else leads us into sin. So to escape the harmful effects of sinful behavior, we've got to go back to what we worship. And the First Commandment is all about God being first.

Consider discovering the "idols" you have in life. Here are three diagnostic questions to help discover what you worship:

1. What do you feel you need in order for life to be good?

2. What makes life worth living?

3. When you dream about the future, what do you dream about obtaining?

Another way we can learn about the idols in our lives is by watching where we turn when we are in trouble.

What are some common things we turn to for comfort and convenience?

We don't get rid of idols just by "being good" or "stopping the bad behavior." What do you think happens when our focus is only on changing behavior and not on getting back to the root causes of our sin?

3 A Vision of the One True God

We've looked at the First Commandment and the meaning of idolatry, so what is the solution? After all, we're often guilty of putting other gods before God. None of us has loved God with exclusive devotion. So what can help us defeat our idols and love God the way He intends?

Look at how Moses described the giving of the Ten Commandments. In this passage from Deuteronomy 5, we notice a connection between getting a glimpse of God in His glory and the desire to get rid of idols.

> 22 "The LORD spoke these commands in a loud voice to your entire assembly from the fire, cloud, and thick darkness on the mountain; He added nothing more. He wrote them on two stone tablets and gave them to me. 23 All of you approached me with your tribal leaders and elders when you heard the voice from the darkness and while the mountain was blazing with fire. 24 You said, 'Look, the LORD our God has shown us His glory and greatness, and we have heard His voice from the fire. Today we have seen that God speaks with a person, yet he still lives. 25 But now, why should we die? This great fire will consume us and we will die if we hear the voice of the LORD our God any longer. 26 For who out of all mankind has heard the voice of the living God speaking from the fire, as we have, and lived? 27 Go near and listen to everything the LORD our God says. Then you can tell us everything the LORD our God tells you; we will listen and obey.'"
> **DEUTERONOMY 5:22-27**

Why were the Israelites inclined to obey God when they received the tablets? Their obedience was connected to their fear of the Lord, and their fear of the Lord was connected to the awesome display of God's power. God had descended upon Mount Sinai, and they had just witnessed His awesome majesty, power, and holiness. Look at these three characteristics of God. They had never previously experienced anything like this.

God's Majesty. The Israelites got a glimpse of God's bigness through the thunder and earthquakes and lightning that surrounded the mountain. They saw a majestic God who commands the creation.

God's Power. The Israelites got a glimpse of God's power in how He delivered them from Egypt. The 10 plagues took aim at the Egyptian gods. From the Nile River turning to blood to the darkness creeping over all of Egypt, God showed He was stronger than the made-up Egyptian deities.

God's Holiness. The Israelites also got a glimpse of God's unassailable holiness. In the passage, you can sense the fear and dread of the people to approach or touch the mountain. God's presence was not just about His power and authority but His perfect righteousness that exposes all our sin.

> What is the relationship between the fear of the Lord and obedience? Is fear of the Lord alone a proper motivation for obedience? Why or why not?

Look at Deuteronomy 5:6: "I am the LORD your God, who brought you out of the land of Egypt, out of the place of slavery." Yes, He is the God who spoke the worlds, the stars, and the galaxies into existence. Yes, He is the God who is so absolutely holy that, apart from grace, no sinful being can survive in His presence. But He is also the God who sent His Son to earth to bear your punishment and save us. He is the mighty Father who carried us in His arms out of the jaws of death.

The power of breaking through patterns of idolatry comes from holding these two truths together: (1) God in all His glory, infinite in size, power, and holiness, and (2) God in Christ humbling Himself to death on a cross for our salvation. When the people of Israel witnessed the glory of God firsthand, the attraction to lesser, inferior, powerless gods was broken. It was the redeeming work of a holy God that led the Israelites to desire to obey God, and it is the redeeming work of Christ on the cross that empowers us to obey God today.

> How is our vision of the one true God transformed by Christ's work on the cross? In what ways can we put on display God's love for the lost?

If breaking free of idolatry comes by gaining a proper vision of God's glory and grace, then the church should display God's glory and grace before a lost world.

> What are some practical ways your group can show others that God is glorious and good?

GROUP STUDY

Warm Up

The First Commandment is about God having first place in your life. It's easy to diagnose idolatry if we are bowing down to statues. But it's more difficult detect subtle ways in which we commit idolatry before God. It's a matter of probing the heart and asking the right questions. Think about these questions you can ask yourself everyday:

- What do you value the most in life?

- What do you love most in life?

- What are you committed to first and foremost?

- What do you trust in the most?

- What commands your obedience?

   Discuss a time when you had an idol in your life. How would these questions work together to seek out such idols? How can we graciously help others see the truth about the idols in their own lives?

   How does ignoring the First Commandment affect your understanding and obedience to all the other commandments?

Identifying what we value the most will increase our clarity as we diagnose the "idols" in our lives. Through prayer and meditation, we can see the relationship between love and trust—these affect our emotions. We can connect the dots between commitment and obedience—these are issues associated with volition and will. And all of these are spiritual matters that engage our mind, heart, and will.

Discussion

Keeping God first in all of life is a continual process. It's not a one-time decision. It's not a self-perpetuating attitude we put on "auto-pilot." It's an ongoing spiritual activity that we practice. It's a habit we development day-by-day. During this time you will have an opportunity to discuss what God revealed to you during the week. Listed below are some of the questions from your daily reading assignments. They will guide your small-group discussion.

1. Think about how God's law and God's love work together for the good of His people. How have you experienced this in your own life?

2. How does our view of commands or rules change when they are separated from personal relationship?

3. Love and exclusivity aren't at odds with each other. God's demand for loyalty is God's display of love. Why is it appropriate for God to demand first place in our lives?

4. Another way we can learn about the idols in our lives is by watching where we turn when we are in trouble. What are some common places or things we turn to for comfort and convenience?

5. We don't get rid of idols just by "being good" or "stopping the bad behavior." What do you think happens when our focus is only on changing behavior and not on getting back to the root causes of our sin?

6. How is our vision of the one true God transformed by Christ's work on the cross? In what ways can we put on display God's love for the lost?

7. If breaking free of idolatry comes by gaining a proper vision of God's glory and grace, then the church should display God's glory and grace before a lost world. What are some practical ways your group can show others that God is glorious and good?

Conclusion

If we are to keep the First Commandment, we must return again and again to the vision of the one true God. The mountain of Sinai points forward to the mountain of Calvary, where Jesus showed the full extent of God's love for the world. This mighty God has given His Son for our redemption, and He has given us His Spirit to empower us to be on mission—leading others to "behold our God." We don't take to the world a list of commandments to follow. We take a gospel of redeeming love through the death and resurrection of Jesus. Only after beholding the beauty and wonder of the gospel are we freed from our idols to serve the one true God.

Spend some time praying this for you and for your group:

"God, I give You permission to reveal any idols in my life.
I don't want to practice idolatry anymore. I want to worship You
alone. You take first place in my mind, heart, and will."

1. Winfield Bevins, *Creed* (Colorado Springs: NavPress, 2011), 98.
2. Martin Luther, *The Large Catechism* (Milton Keynes, UK: Authentic Media Limited, 2012).

It is the intent of this commandment to require
true faith and trust of the heart which settles upon
the only true God and clings to Him alone.[2]

MARTIN LUTHER

NOTES

THE GOSPEL PROJECT

Session 4

God First in Revealing Himself

If you uproot the idol and fail to plant the love of Christ in its place, the idol will grow back.[1]

TIMOTHY KELLER

INDIVIDUAL STUDY

"Do not make an idol for yourself" (Ex. 20:4). The majority of people probably don't pay much attention to the Second Commandment for a couple of reasons. First, Christians in Western cultures have abandoned the notion of carving, fashioning, or making any physical image of God to worship. For the most part, the ancient idea of fashioning little figurines to which we can worship and pray simply does not exist.

But the second reason sounds similar and is based on the first. Christians in Western cultures have forgotten that there are different ways to "carve out images" of God—mentally, emotionally, and intellectually. The ancient idea may have disappeared, but the problem of "imagining our own God" will always be a contemporary one. The Second Commandment is broken regularly by people inside and outside the church. This kind of disobedience has devastating consequences for us and our families.

What are some ways people may seek to "improve" upon the God of the Bible?

Why do you think God forbids us to make images that reflect Him?

The First Commandment is about giving our allegiance to something or someone other than the true God. The Second is about trying to turn the true God into something else. It's about trying to "improve" God by fashioning Him in our own image.

In the Second Commandment, God condemns idolatry because of His passionate jealousy for our worship. Idolatry is dangerous because it distorts our view of God and corrupts our behavior, leading us away from God as He has revealed Himself and toward a false god who is powerless to save and transform us. In order to engage in God's mission, we need the power that comes from a Spirit-transformed heart.

This week engage the daily study sections associated with *God First* as a way to better understand God's desire for our worship and attention. Interact with the daily reading and the Scriptures, and be ready to discuss with your small group.

God is Jealous for Our Worship

In the previous session, we saw how God reminded His people of His relationship with them. He is the God who rescued them from slavery and made them His own special people. His First Commandment was about exclusivity—we can have no other gods besides Him. In the Second Commandment, God forbids the wrong kind of worship:

> [8] Do not make an idol for yourself in the shape of anything in the heavens above or on the earth below or in the waters under the earth. [9] You must not bow down to them or worship them, because I, the Lord your God, am a jealous God, punishing the children for the fathers' sin to the third and fourth generations of those who hate Me, [10] but showing faithful love to a thousand generations of those who love Me and keep My commands.
> DEUTERONOMY 5:8-10

Our first reaction when reading this passage may be one of relief. You may think, "Whew! Thank God I've never made an idol with my hands or bowed down to a statue!" But the idolatry condemned in this Commandment is more than merely crafting a statue to represent God. It's about making God in our image rather than realizing we are made in His image. In other words, we break the Second Commandment whenever we define God in our hearts as we want Him to be instead of believing what He has revealed Himself to be.

God gets to define Himself. We aren't the creators of an imaginary god, rather the creation of the true God who has revealed Himself. We must conform to the truth about God rather than Him into what we think we would like for Him to be.

Suppose a writer wanted his next book to be a biography about you. You are flattered at first. But after the book is written, you discover that the writer has described you as an astronaut who has a terrible time with relationships. And the book ends with you living alone with 18 cats. You approach the writer and point out his errors. But he only smiles and replies, "But this is how I prefer to see you. I find you much more interesting this way." Not only would you be offended, but you would have the right to be. The author has ignored the truth and preferred a different version of you—implying that he doesn't like you the way you really are!

The Second Commandment, in a much greater sense, gets to this very issue between us and God. God is saying, "You cannot prefer to see Me your way. You are not allowed to remake Me into what you want Me to be. I AM WHO I AM."

Have you ever heard the phrase, "My God is like ..." or "My God would never do ..."? What do these phrases communicate about our view of God?

In what ways do you think God's prohibition of idolatry helps protect His people?

God demands to be rightly represented because God is jealous for our worship. His jealousy is different than the jealousy we feel as human beings. God's jealousy is rooted in His love for His glory and His love for His people. God knows that when we worship Him for who He is, we will find joy and satisfaction in Him. And because God wants us to find our joy in Him, He forbids us to worship a figment of our imagination.

God gets first shot at revealing Himself. Once we begin forming an image of God based on who we'd like Him to be rather than who He is, we are breaking the Second Commandment. We make assumptions about God and then project those assumptions onto Him. And when He doesn't act on those assumptions, we get angry and disappointed. At the end of the day, God wants us to know Him and make Him known. So when we break the Second Commandment, we rob ourselves of the joy of really knowing God. In all of this, we are no longer relying on what God has revealed about Himself. Instead, we are revealing what our sinful hearts want to believe. Ultimately, we set ourselves up to fail.

Why is it important that our opinions about God match up with the reality of God's revelation of Himself?

What are common "graven images" in our lives and thoughts today?

What are some books, movies, and television shows that portray God in one form or another? What kind of influence does this have on you, family, church, or culture?

Idols Distort Our View of God

As Moses was receiving the Ten Commandments for the first time, the children of Israel had already gone about breaking them. How ironic! The account of the Israelites worshiping the golden calf is a vivid illustration of the dangers of idolatry.

Take a look at the scene described in Exodus 32. Moses has gone up the mountain to commune with God and to receive instruction for the people. As the days pass by, the Israelites begin to worry about Moses' whereabouts, which leads them to make this request:

> [1] When the people saw that Moses delayed in coming down from the mountain, they gathered around Aaron and said to him, "Come, make us a god who will go before us because this Moses, the man who brought us up from the land of Egypt—we don't know what has happened to him!" [2] Then Aaron replied to them, "Take off the gold rings that are on the ears of your wives, your sons, and your daughters and bring them to me." [3] So all the people took off the gold rings that were on their ears and brought them to Aaron. [4] He took the gold from their hands, fashioned it with an engraving tool, and made it into an image of a calf. Then they said, "Israel, this is your God, who brought you up from the land of Egypt!"
>
> EXODUS 32:1-4

Let's unpack this scenario. First, we see that the people were worrying about Moses and their future. They were wandering in the wilderness. They are susceptible to enemy attack and concerned about their survival. Even though they just witnessed God destroy the Egyptian army in the Red Sea, they doubted the power of God.

So what did they request? Not a new god but an image of God they could see and touch. They wanted something tangible, something to give them comfort and go before them. The bull was something God had told them to sacrifice in worship to Him. To ancient people, the bull represented strength.

What better attribute of God to cling on to during uncertain times and difficult circumstances? And what better way to represent God's strength than to make a bull that would guarantee their protection? This distorted image of God came from frightened hearts. The people of Israel were worried, and they failed to trust God. Right here, we see idolatry on full display.

When we're worried and insecure, we seek to shape our view of God in a way that brings us comfort, hoping that this image of God will guarantee our future peace and happiness. Instead of seeing God for who He is, we end up seeing Him as our idolatrous, dysfunctional heart wants Him to be. God becomes simply a reflection of us and a reflection of our idolatry.

What are some reasons why our hearts rush to the making of idols?

In what ways can our view of God become distorted by our idolatry?

What does it mean to use God?

The problem with making a graven image of God is that it can only show you one dimension of God. It will never express all of Him. And once we latch on to only one aspect of God, we end up distorting who God actually is.

For example if you drew a picture of God, would you draw Him smiling or frowning? If you draw Him smiling, you might capture His goodness and fatherliness but not His wrath against sin. If you draw Him frowning, you might capture His anger against sin, but you wouldn't show His grace and forgiveness. If you draw Him towering above the heavens, you obscure the fact that He is close to us and shares intimately in our pain. But if you show Him as a friend by your side, you obscure the fact that He's the God of infinite majesty and worth and unspeakable holiness. That's the problem with pictures of God. They always conceal more than they reveal. They distort more than they reflect.

How have you reduced God down to a single attribute? In what ways did this "lopsided" view of God affect your life, your walk with Him, the decisions you make?

3 Idols Corrupt Our Behavior

The story doesn't end with a distorted view of God. As we read on, we see how a corrupted vision of God leads to corrupted behavior.

> [5] When Aaron saw this, he built an altar before it; then he made an announcement: "There will be a festival to the Lord tomorrow." [6] Early the next morning they arose, offered burnt offerings, and presented fellowship offerings. The people sat down to eat and drink, then got up to play.
> [7] The Lord spoke to Moses: "Go down at once! For your people you brought up from the land of Egypt have acted corruptly. [8] They have quickly turned from the way I commanded them; they have made for themselves an image of a calf. They have bowed down to it, sacrificed to it, and said, 'Israel, this is your God, who brought you up from the land of Egypt.' "
> EXODUS 32:5-8

The event began as a worship festival in honor of the Lord, and it ended with a raucous party of immorality. "The people sat down to eat and drink, then got up to play" (v. 6). In Hebrew the word *play* can have sexual connotations to it. God told Moses to go back down the mountain because the people were stiff-necked and hard-hearted. They had quickly corrupted themselves.

An important point can be made here. The children of Israel created an image that gave them a distorted vision of God. They worshiped this depiction of God for less than a day before they were involved in immoral behavior. Idolatry distorts our vision and then corrupts our behavior. And when we trace our sinful behavior backward, we'll often find a distorted vision of God.

What is the relationship between our view of God and our behavior?
What are some choices we make that come from a wrong view of God?

True spiritual growth comes from seeing and knowing God—all of Him, not part of Him. If you focus on only one dimension of God, you'll grow in a deformed way. Your life won't reflect the goodness, holiness, and mercy of God the way He intends. Here are some examples:

- If you view God only as holy and just, you may tend to be judgmental and impatient.

- If you view God only as gracious and loving, you may tend to treat sin casually.

- If you view God as a distant Judge, you may assume He is mad at you whenever things go wrong.

- If you view God as One who guarantees prosperity, then you will be disillusioned when things go wrong.

Do you see how our view of God leads to different kinds of behavior? The patterns in our life can be traced back to our understanding of who God is. Look for the places of stress, anxiety, and dissatisfaction in your life, the places where you're most tempted to sin, and then trace them back to a wrong view of God.

Here's the point. Are you worried? Embrace God's sovereignty. Are you insecure? Embrace the fact that in Christ you have the absolute approval and affirmation of the God who created the universe. He loves you tenderly as a Father. Are you judgmental? Think about how much mercy God has shown you. Are you stingy? Consider how generous God has been with you. Are you materialistic? Think about how much more beautiful God is than money. Embrace all of God and who He is.

The Bible teaches that we become like what we worship. Jeremiah 2:5 says that when we worship worthless things, we become worthless. When we worship money, we become materialistic and anxious all the time about our savings. When we worship family, we become codependent and obsessive about our children. When we worship romance, we become possessive in our relationships. Whatever it is you worship, you reflect.

How does our view of God impact the way we treat others?

Why is idolatry a hindrance to our mission and message as Christians?

God reveals Himself in words because pictures and images can never contain Him. Pictures and images conceal more than they reveal. But thankfully, in only one place can you see a picture of God. Colossians 1:15 says that Jesus "is the image of the invisible God." Hebrews 1:3 offers that the Son is "the exact expression of His nature." We see the real God in the life, death, and resurrection of Jesus. In Him, we see God in all His glory.

GROUP STUDY

Warm Up

Let those who worship stones be ashamed. Because those stones were dead, we have found a living Stone; indeed those stones never lived, so that they cannot be called even dead; but our Stone is living, and hath ever lived with the Father, and though He died for us, He revived, and liveth now, and death shall no more have dominion over Him.[2]

AUGUSTINE (354-430)

The only way to free ourselves from the destructive influence of counterfeit gods is to turn back to the true one. The living God, who revealed himself both at Mount Sinai and on the Cross, is the only Lord who, if you find him, can truly fulfill you, and, if you fail him, can truly forgive you.[3]

TIMOTHY KELLER

Which quote resonates with you the most? Explain.

John Stott gives four expressions of idolatry. All of which minimizes "the gulf between the Creator and his creatures, in order to bring him under our control."

1. " To localize God—confining him within limits which we impose, whereas he is the Creator of the universe.

2. To domesticate God—making him dependent on us, taming and taping him, whereas he is the Sustainer of human life.

3. To alienate God—blaming him for his distance and his silence, whereas he is the Ruler of nations, and not far from any of us.

4. To dethrone God, demoting him to some image of our own contrivance or craft, whereas he is our Father from whom we derive our being."[4]

Which of the four different expressions of idolatry have you experienced? How do you avoid moving to an extreme and remain centered?

Discussion

You know what it's like to walk out of a movie theater into the daylight, right? The light hurts our eyes to the point we have to shield them. Why? It's because our eyes are used to darkness. At first it hurts to walk into the sunlight. But once we stay in the light, our eyes refocus. We are able to see the light and all that it reveals. The sunlight doesn't change to accommodate us! Our eyes adjust to take in all that the sun reveals.

This is how we rid ourselves of idols. God works on your heart because we are walking in the light. We don't shield our eyes and turn away. We embrace God's Word and what His truth exposes. During this group time, take some time to "walk in the light." Discuss what God revealed to you during the week. Here are some of the questions from your daily reading assignments. Take some time to share with each other.

1. In what ways do you think God's prohibition of idolatry helps protect His people?

2. What are some reasons why our hearts rush to the making of idols? In what ways can our view of God become distorted by our idolatry?

3. What are some books, movies, and television shows that portray God in one form or another? What kind of influence does this have on you, family, church, or culture?

4. In what ways have you reduced God down to a single attribute? How did this "lopsided" view of God affect your life, your walk with Him, the decisions you make?

5. What is the relationship between our view of God and our behavior? What are some choices we make that come from a wrong view of God?

6. How does our view of God impact the way we treat others? Why is idolatry a hindrance to our mission and message as Christians?

Conclusion

Idolatry isn't just about statues, trinkets, superstition, or physical carvings. It's about accepting and embracing all of God for who He is. That means we rid ourselves of any incorrect "image" we have in our minds. This, too, is a journey for each believer as we grow in our relationship with God.

Idolatry is dangerous because it distorts our view of God and corrupts our behavior. It leads us away from God as He has revealed Himself and toward a false god who is powerless to save and transform us. In order to engage in God's mission, we need the power that comes from a Spirit-transformed heart. The answer to idolatry isn't more willpower, knowledge, Bible study, or church attendance. It's Jesus. The graven images fall away in light of the true image of God, who shows us the light of His glory.

Spend some time praying this for you and for your group:

"God, help me see You for who You really are! I need you to change my heart by the power of Your Holy Spirit through a dynamic relationship with Your Son. I yield any and all preconceived ideas and 'images' of You at the altar of my heart. Change me so I can serve You for the world's good and for Your glory!"

1. Timothy Keller, *Counterfeit Gods: The Empty Promises of Money, Sex, Power, and the Only Hope that Matters* (New York: Penguin Group, 2009), 172.
2. Augustine, *On the Psalms, in Nicene and Post-Nicene Fathers*, First Series, ed. Philip Schaff, vol. 8 (New York: Cosimo, reprinted 2007), 477.
3. Timothy Keller, *Counterfeit Gods: The Empty Promises of Money, Sex, Power, and the Only Hope that Matters* (New York: Penguin Group, 2009), XXIV.
4. John Stott, *The Message of Acts* (Downers Grove, IL: InterVarsity Press, 1994), 287.
5. Kyle Idleman, *Gods at War* (Grand Rapids: Zondervan, 2013), 49.

> You can't understand the seriousness of idolatry without understanding the jealousy of God. And you can't understand his jealousy without some understanding of his relentless, powerful love for you, because they are intertwined.[5]
>
> KYLE IDLEMAN

NOTES

THE **GOSPEL** PROJECT.

Session 5

God First in Name and Renown

"Yes, Yahweh, we wait for You
in the path of Your judgments.
Our desire is for Your name and renown."

ISAIAH 26:8

INDIVIDUAL STUDY

What's in a name? A name is something bestowed upon us before or at birth, an aspect of our identity that comes from outside ourselves. Like it or not, your name comes from your parents, and changing it can be a difficult process. When we give a child a name, we exercise our authority. A baby boy doesn't name himself. The baby isn't in charge. Parents exercise authority by giving names to their children.

There is a link between an individual *name* and our reputation *in name*. That's why we use the word name to refer to how others see us—"He has a good name," or "She doesn't live up to her name." People have often said that it takes a lifetime to build up a good name but only a few minutes to destroy it.

> **Do you know the story behind your name? To what degree are you conscious of your reputation—the meaning of your name? Why?**

The meaning and significance of names can change over time. Throughout the 1990s, one of the most popular names given to American girls was Monica. But in 1998, the name dropped to the bottom of the Top 100 Names for girls. And in 1999 it disappeared off the list altogether. The decline in popularity for the name Monica took place at the time the Monica Lewinsky scandal was threatening the presidency of Bill Clinton. Parents shied away from the name because of its contemporary connotations. A beautiful name was temporarily tarnished by a political scandal.

Concerning the Third Commandment, it's no surprise then to see why God forbids us to take His name in vain. God's name is worthy of all honor. Breaking this Commandment brings punishment because of the weightiness of God's glory. The good news is that Jesus Christ has perfectly hallowed God's name. And through Jesus' accomplished work on the cross, we are forgiven and empowered to spread the fame of God's name to a lost world.

Throughout the week engage these daily study sections on your own. Each of these readings revolve around different aspects of the Third Commandment, and they will help you prepare for your small-group discussion. Interact with the Scriptures, and be ready to interact with your small group.

1 God's Name is Worthy of All Honor

Just as parents exert their authority by giving their child a name, so also God exerted His authority when He made us in His image. God called us human. In Hebrew the word *Adam* means *human* or *humanity*. When God fashioned the first man from the dust of the ground, He had a name in mind. We don't name God; He names us. This is an expression of His authority.

But God has also expressed a desire for relationship with His creation. That's one reason why God revealed His name as Yahweh, which means "I AM WHO I AM." The name "I AM" tells us something about God—about His transcendence, His eternal nature, the force and weight of His being.

So we see that God has expressed His authority over us by naming us. But He has also expressed His desire for friendship with us by revealing to us His name. Whenever you strike up a conversation with a stranger, you often begin by discussing common elements of whatever situation in which you find yourselves. But an invisible barrier comes down when you say, "My name is …" and extend your hand. You move from chitchat to more personal knowledge.

What is the significance of God revealing His name to His people?

What does God's name tell us about His character and attributes?

God revealed His name in an act of holy friendship with His people. The Jewish people revered His name so much that they often refrained from uttering it—choosing to use the Hebrew word *hashem*. This word simply means *the Name* and using it was shorthand for referring to God.

For this reason, you can find all kinds of references to God's "Name" in the Scriptures. Psalm 20, for example, encourages us to trust in the name of the Lord for protection. The name of the Lord is to be feared (see Ps. 102:15), but it's also a refuge, a strong tower in which we can find safety (see Prov. 18:10). By the time we get to the prophets, we see the name of the Lord being described as on the move, coming from afar, burning with His anger against evil (see Isa. 30:27). Micah referred to God's name as a realm in which we are to walk. "Though all the peoples each walk in the name of their gods, we will walk in the name of Yahweh our God forever and ever" (Mic. 4:5). Jesus Himself picked up on this theme as He urged His followers to abide in Him for life (see John 15:5).

God is big into His name! He is filled with zeal and jealousy for it. So it should be no surprise that He forcefully condemns the misuse of His name in the Third Commandment:

> Do not misuse the name of the Lord your God, because the Lord
> will not leave anyone unpunished who misuses His name.
> DEUTERONOMY 5:11

One of the main reasons we are told not to misuse God's name is because His name is powerful. How many job opportunities come up because you have access to someone's name? You put down a well-known, respected person as a personal reference. Or you ask an honored individual with a sphere of influence to put in a good word for you. It's great when someone says, "Just tell them I sent you." The personal contact makes all the difference. You are being granted access to the power that comes from that name.

The beautiful truth of Scripture is that God allows us to know Him by name. We are given access to the God who made heaven and earth. We are strengthened by the name of the Lord.

Unfortunately, we are also tempted to use the power of a person's name in the wrong way. Some people will make it seem like they are closer to power and influence than they really are. They start "name-dropping" make it appear they have a personal connection to someone prominent. When it comes to the name of God, sometimes we use it for our own will and purposes. Maybe we use God's name to further our own agenda, or win an argument, or gain the honor of religious men. Instead of bowing to God's name to keep it holy, we use (or abuse) the name of God as a means to a greater end.

What are some ways God's name is misused in the world? Why does God take this so seriously?

What are some names God uses to reveal Himself in Scripture?

What are some names that God's people have used to describe Him?

2 God Will Not Overlook Blasphemy

The Fifth Commandment ("Honor your father and your mother") comes with a promise. The Third Commandment, however, comes with a punishment. God doesn't overlook blasphemy, and neither should His people. In fact, in Leviticus 24, we see just how seriously God's people took this command:

> [10] Now the son of an Israelite mother and an Egyptian father was among the Israelites. A fight broke out in the camp between the Israelite woman's son and an Israelite man. [11] Her son cursed and blasphemed the Name, and they brought him to Moses. (His mother's name was Shelomith, a daughter of Dibri of the tribe of Dan.) [12] They put him in custody until the Lord's decision could be made clear to them. [13] Then the Lord spoke to Moses: [14] "Bring the one who has cursed to the outside of the camp and have all who heard him lay their hands on his head; then have the whole community stone him. [15] And tell the Israelites: If anyone curses his God, he will bear the consequences of his sin. [16] Whoever blasphemes the name of Yahweh is to be put to death; the whole community must stone him. If he blasphemes the Name, he is to be put to death, whether the foreign resident or the native. [23] After Moses spoke to the Israelites, they brought the one who had cursed to the outside of the camp and stoned him. So the Israelites did as the Lord had commanded Moses.
>
> LEVITICUS 24:10-16,23

In a contemporary "civilized" culture, we may see this kind of punishment as excessive. But we would do well to remind ourselves that the wages of sin is death (see Rom. 6:23). And Hebrew civilization in ancient times was a theocracy. This is God's law for His people. God dealt with His people in concrete terms—showing how serious sins merited immediate serious consequences. The punishment seen here only underscores the weightiness of the offense.

What does the severity of punishment for breaking the Third Commandment tell us about God's view of His own importance?

We misuse the name of the Lord in many ways—flippantly, untruthfully, and hypocritically.

Flippantly. Using God's name by cursing and swearing certainly fall into this category. Think of the ways we use God's name without giving Him the reverence He deserves. When we say these things, we're making it seem as if God is the One who damns others according to our own wishes. Conversely, if we use the phrases like "God bless you" without sincerity, it could also be considered a misuse of God's name.

> **What are some examples of trivializing God's name that you have witnessed? How can we deepen our respect for God's name?**

Untruthfully. When we speak about God in ways that are not true, we discredit Him and tarnish His reputation. Consider the importance of your own name. When someone gossips or spreads lies about you, the natural response is to seek to restore your name. Now magnify your sense of jealousy for your name millions of times, and you begin to see why God is so adamant that His name be used in truthful and honorable ways. Using God's name untruthfully can also include misrepresenting Him and His will. It's what happens when people attach God's name to something when it actually goes against God's Word—apartheid in South Africa, Christians who upheld slavery, Nazism in Germany, the Crusades.

> **What are some examples of untrue words about God that you have heard? How can we ensure that we're speaking the truth about God and not lies?**

Hypocritically. How does God show what He is like to the rest of the world? Yes, He does it through His Word, creation, and conscience. But God reveals Himself to others through His people. The apostle John wrote to a friend, "You will do well to send them on their journey in a manner worthy of God, since they set out for the sake of the Name" (3 John 6-7). We carry around Christ's name everywhere we go. Our manner of life should demonstrate the worthiness of God's name. To misuse it is to act hypocritically in ways that damage the testimony of God.

> **How do you take God's name in vain the most?**

> **How can we support each other in obeying the Third Commandment?**

3 Make the Name of Jesus Known

> The New Testament is not silent about ... the frivolous use of
> God's name. Reverence for God and His name is still prevalent
> in the New Testament. However, the stress is often shifted
> to the name of Jesus, God incarnate. We are now to believe
> in the name of Jesus (John 1:12), be baptized in the name of
> Jesus (Acts 8:16), and worship in the name of Jesus (Acts
> 9:14). There is no other name by which we are saved (Acts
> 4:12). For His is the name above all names. Every knee will
> bow and every tongue confess that He is Lord (Phil. 2:9-11).[1]

MARK F. ROOKER

According to the Law, we all deserve the fate of the man we read about in Leviticus. The Third Commandment should drive us to our knees where we ask and receive mercy that comes from the gospel. There is One who has never misused God's name. In fact, He upheld and lifted up God's name in all He said and did. Jesus honored God's name as holy. And in the Lord's Prayer, He called us to pray that God would hallow His name:

> He said to them, "Whenever you pray, say: 'Father, Your
> name be honored as holy. Your kingdom come.'"
> LUKE 11:2

Do you see how this request is given in the third person? The prayer is not to us but to God. May Your name be honored as holy. May Your name be hallowed. Of course, the expectation is that those of us who pray for God's name to be made holy would, in turn, speak and act in ways that further that end. But implicit in the prayer is the idea that God Himself would honor His name as holy so that the world will be filled with the glory He deserves. In other words, "God, You do this! I can't do this. But I know that You can do this through me!"

It's the Father who brings God's kingdom, provides daily provision, announces forgiveness from sins, and delivers us from the Evil One. He accomplishes all of these things through Jesus Christ His Son. It is the Father who hallows His name through the work of His Son. By His life and death Jesus hallowed God's name—showing us what God is like. Jesus came into this world as the perfect representation of God.

How did Jesus hallow God's name through His life and ministry?

What are some ways we can hallow God's name in the world?
Together as the church?

We don't hallow the name of God just by "avoiding" the misuse of His name. Christians carry the name of Jesus Christ in power and ministry to the world. We read about the early church and find multiple references to the power of Jesus' name. Peter declared that salvation comes from calling upon the name of the Lord (see Acts 2:21). He instructed the crowds at Pentecost to be baptized in the name of Jesus for forgiveness. Peter performed miracles in the name of Jesus Christ (see Acts 3:6; 4:10,30), and the religious leaders felt threatened to the point they asked the apostles no longer to preach in Jesus' name (see 4:18; 5:40). Even when they were persecuted for preaching the gospel, the apostles rejoiced that they were "counted worthy to be dishonored on behalf of the Name" (5:41).

What is the significance of the power of Jesus' name for our mission?

How does our desire to spread the fame of Christ connect to our mission
as Christ's disciples?

GROUP STUDY

Warm Up

Names are important because they identify us and represent our reputation. Identity theft is a serious crime because it is representing oneself under the guise of another in order to gain access to confidential and privileged information. You guard your name because your name represents your life.

Have you ever experienced someone using your name in a way you did not approve? How did you respond?

Why is it important to rightly understand the value of God's name?

Understanding the value of God's name helps us understand why and how He vindicates His name. We see the gospel story come to fruition with the advent of Jesus Christ—the Son of God who inherited the name above all names.

Discussion

Take some time to discuss what God revealed to you during the week. Listed below are some of the questions from your daily reading assignments. They will guide your small-group discussion. Ask God to continue to teach you how He defends and justifies His name throughout history in all the earth.

1. Do you know the story behind your name? To what degree are you conscience of your reputation—the meaning of your name? Why?

2. What are some ways God's name is misused in the world? What about in the church? Why do you think God takes this so seriously?

3. What are some names God uses to reveal Himself in Scripture? What are some names that God's people have used to describe Him?

4. Which of the ways of taking God's name in vain do you struggle with the most? In what ways can we support each other in obeying the Third Commandment?

5. How did Jesus hallow God's name through His life and ministry? What are some ways we can hallow God's name in the world? Together as the church?

6. What is the significance of the power of Jesus' name for our mission? How does our desire to spread the fame of Christ connect to our mission as Christ's disciples?

Conclusion

Making famous the name of God revealed in Jesus Christ is the mission of the church. In our words and works, we are to witness to the One who hallowed God's name perfectly and gave us His salvation as a gift. Unlike publicity agents who puff up the name and reputation of humans for earthly gain, we speak to the truth of Christ's name and seek to spread His fame and glory for heavenly gain.

Spend some time praying this for you and for your group:

> "God, I refuse to use Your name without honor and meaning. I don't want to be the person that uses your name for greater gain. Help me be the Christ follower that is used by You to make Your name great! May my life bring glory and honor to You—drawing attention to Your work of redemption through Your Son, Jesus Christ."

1. Mark Rooker, *The Ten Commandments: Ethics for the Twenty-First Century* (Nashville: B&H Publishing, 2010), 71.
2. John Wesley, "Upon our Lord's Sermon on the Mount, Discourse IV," in *John Wesley's Sermons: An Anthology*, eds. Albert Outler and Richard Heitzenrater (Nashville: Abingdon Press, 1991), 203.

In praying that God, or "his name," may "be hallowed" or glorified, we pray that he may be known, such as he is.[2]

JOHN WESLEY

NOTES

THE GOSPEL PROJECT

God First in Our Work and Rest

In a very real sense, the idea of the Sabbath pulls humanity out of its self-interest and striving. It presses people to find contentment in the idea that God is ultimately in control and does, in fact, provide for the needs that too often they find themselves attempting to fulfill on their own during the work week.[1]

TIMOTHY M. PIERCE

INDIVIDUAL STUDY

Have you ever worked so long and worn yourself out so much that you just had to get away for some rest and relaxation? So you make a plan, schedule some time off, set an agenda, and take a vacation. But once you come back to the daily grind, you find yourself thinking, *I need to take a vacation from my vacation.* Or maybe after coming back from your holiday break, your friends ask, "How was your vacation?" You know the answer because it was busy. You chronicle all the activities from packing to traveling. You take an inventory of how you spent your time. What's the conclusion? It may have been a holiday, but it was no vacation!

> **What's the busiest time of the year for you? How do you handle the hustle and bustle of your personal calendar?**

> **Think about the rhythm of your own daily grind. What drains you more than anything? What seems to fill you up?**

All of us desire rest from our work. Some call it "me time." We always seem to come up a little short at the end of our time off. We wake up to go back to work. Monday rolls around yet again.

In the Gospels Jesus said, "All of you, take up My yoke and learn from Me, because I am gentle and humble in heart, and you will find rest for yourselves. For My yoke is easy and My burden is light" (Matt. 11:29-30). This offer sounds too good to be true. Rest for my soul? This promise from Christ is rooted in the Fourth Commandment—remember the Sabbath day to keep it holy. This is another way in which Jesus reveals Himself as the One who not only perfectly kept the law, but also fulfills the law. Jesus isn't offering rest as a by-product of following Him. Jesus is the rest. He is the fulfillment of the Sabbath law. Without Christ, we will work even while we are resting. But with Christ, we will rest even while we are working.

In the Fourth Commandment, God established the Sabbath as a way for His people to refocus their relationship on Him, rest from their labors, and remember His work in creation and redemption. Jesus fulfilled the Sabbath through His death and resurrection. By observing the principle of the Sabbath, we remember our identity in Christ and are empowered for His mission.

This week engage the daily study sections associated with God First as a way to better understand Jesus and our relationship with Him and the Sabbath. Interact with the daily reading and the Scriptures, and be ready to discuss with your small group.

1 The Sabbath: To Refocus

The Ten Commandments are listed first in Exodus 20. The nation of Israel had just been led out of Egypt by Moses, and God gave him the law on Mount Sinai. When Moses repeated the Commandments in Deuteronomy (literally, "second law"), he was doing so forty years later. Consider it the "highlights" of the law with "commentary of what's really important." Moses has sprinkled his notes throughout the book making clarifications for God's people. They have been wandering through the desert for a generation. Regarding the Sabbath Commandment, he begins:

> Be careful to remember the Sabbath day, to keep it holy
> as the Lord your God has commanded you.
> **DEUTERONOMY 5:12**

By "remember the Sabbath," Moses says, "observe the Sabbath." This doesn't mean to just remember that God gave a Sabbath day of rest. It means we are actually to observe a Sabbath day of rest. We are to keep this day "holy," or set apart because that's what God did with it. At the conclusion of the creation week in Genesis 1, God "completed His work that He had done, and He rested on the seventh day from all His work that He had done. God blessed the seventh day and declared it holy, for on it He rested from His work of creation" (Gen. 2:2-3). So, following the pattern of God, we are to set aside a day to rest from our work.

Our work consumes so much of our time. It can easily dominate our lives and push God out of the picture, to the point we end up with work replacing God. How does our work begin to replace God? If we think that our work defines us or provides for us, then we've replaced God with our work. God is supposed to do both of those things. His love for us gives us our identity. His care for us sustains and provides for us.

What are some specific ways you have turned to work to define you and sustain you?

How do you think Sabbath-keeping helps you refocus your mind's attention and heart's affection on God?

All of the Commandments ultimately flow out of the first one, that we have no other gods but God Himself. The Fourth Commandment is given to us to help us make sure that work (which we're consumed with 40-50 hours per week, or more) doesn't replace God as our primary source of identity or security. The First Commandment is the heart of the Fourth Commandment. God wants to make sure that He remains our primary focus, our source of identity, and the Person in whom we trust for provision.

But God says, "I am the source of your identity. I have specially designed you. I have loved you. I have a plan for you." Our identity and worth does not come from our abilities—what we can give to God. No, our identity is found in God's love for us—what He has freely given to us. In other words, we don't earn a day of rest from God because of all that we do for Him. It's just the opposite. We are commanded to take a day of rest because of all that He has done for us. We don't stop and rest to remember how much we have accomplished. We stop and rest to remember the goodness and greatness of God.

What are some ways people define their worth?

What are the benefits of taking a day of rest each week to reflect on God and His goodness?

In your own words, how would you define rest?

What's the difference between rest and relaxation (or leisure)? Can you rest while pursuing leisure?

2 The Sabbath: To Rest and Rely on Him

> [13] You are to labor six days and do all your work, [14] but the seventh
> day is a Sabbath to the LORD your God. You must not do any work—
> you, your son or daughter, your male or female slave, your ox or
> donkey, any of your livestock, or the foreigner who lives within your
> gates, so that your male and female slaves may rest as you do.
> DEUTERONOMY 5:13-14

Because working is the primary instrument God uses to meet our physical needs, we can quickly begin to trust our work rather than God. For this reason, God made the Israelites take one day off each week to do nothing. Even the servants were to rest! Think about the radical shift in their mindset. This was a different experience than that of Egypt. As slaves of the Pharaoh, they were used to the abuse. Seven days a week from sunup to sundown was their daily grind. Now God says, "take a day off … even your own slaves!"

We would think that this Commandment to rest would be gladly received and kept by God's children. But leaving the abuse of Egypt also meant leaving the provision it offered. When survival is too often a day-to-day challenge, it is hard to trust God regardless of your circumstances.

> What kind of "use and abuse" do you feel when you work? Is it self-imposed?

> What are the realistic options for you to make a change for the better?

Consider this paraphrase. So God says, "On the seventh day, do absolutely nothing! Not because you can afford it, but because I want you to have some space where you have to trust Me. I want to fight for you. I want to multiply your efforts and provide miraculously for you. This is My built-in commandment to keep you relying on me."

When we honor the Sabbath day, God multiplies our work on the other six days. Think about this. The Sabbath law cut the Israelites' productivity by one-seventh. That's 14.2%.

That doesn't make much business sense. God doesn't want us running on 100% capacity to provide for ourselves. He wants us relying on Him 100% to provide for us.

Actually, the big picture is whether we trust God at all. This is what lies at the heart of this Commandment. Do we really trust God? Later in Israel's journey we see God drive them into exile under the enemy's rule. God promised this would happen—He basically said "I drove you into exile for not keeping the Sabbath" (see Lev. 26:34-35). They stopped trusting God with the Sabbath, and they suffered the consequences. In a very personal way, keeping the Sabbath represents a whole life that trusts God for everything. When we break the Fourth Commandment, it points to the fact that you don't keep the First Commandment.

Do you take the Sabbath Commandment seriously? Why or why not?

How might Sabbath-keeping be vital for your own spiritual and physical well-being?

How do you think keeping the Sabbath points to the gospel?

In what practical ways does the Sabbath direct you to rely upon God today?

3 The Sabbath: To See God's Goodness

> Remember that you were a slave in the land of Egypt, and the Lord your God
> brought you out of there with a strong hand and an outstretched arm. That
> is why the Lord your God has commanded you to keep the Sabbath day.
> DEUTERONOMY 5:15

Why did God ask His people to remember Egypt? What were they supposed to remember? First, God desired that Israel keep their eyes on Him for provision and rest. But over time, Moses included something else. When he repeated this Commandment in Deuteronomy, Moses expanded the purpose of the Sabbath from remembering God's provision to remembering His redemption.

The Israelites were to take one day a week and remind themselves that they used to be slaves under a cruel master. But in His love, God had compassion on His children and led them out of Egypt. So keeping the Sabbath facilitated their act of remembrance for the redemptive work of God on their behalf.

This same notion is echoed by Paul in the New Testament. In the Book of Colossians, Paul essentially claims that God has done for the Gentile nations (formerly considered enemies of God) the same thing He did for the nation of Israel (the children of God). This redemptive work was accomplished through Jesus Christ and His work on the cross:

> [19] For God was pleased to have
> all His fullness dwell in Him,
> [20] and through Him to reconcile
> everything to Himself
> by making peace
> through the blood of His cross,—
> whether things on earth or things in heaven.
> [21] Once you were alienated and hostile in your minds because of your evil
> actions. [22] But now He has reconciled you by His physical body through
> His death, to present you holy, faultless, and blameless before Him—
> COLOSSIANS 1:19-22

In your own words, what does all of this mean for you today? How do you carve out time from your busy week to remember the redemptive work of God in your life?

The principle of the Sabbath is applied differently in the New Testament than in the Old Testament. Paul explains, "Therefore, don't let anyone judge you in regard to food and drink or in the matter of a festival or a new moon or a Sabbath day" (Col. 2:16). In his Letter to the Romans, Paul writes, "One person considers one day to be above another day. Someone else considers every day to be the same. Each one must be fully convinced in his own mind" (Rom. 14:5).

Consistent throughout his ministry, Paul taught Gentile Christians that they were under no obligation to keep the law (see Gal. 5). This is important to understand. Jesus did not replace or abolish the law (see Matt. 5:17). Rather He came and fulfilled the law. But Jesus' life, death, and resurrection did replace the old covenant (see Heb. 8:7-13). The new covenant is the gospel—the "good news" that we can be reconciled to God though faith in Jesus Christ regardless of ethnic background, race, or religious pedigree. The law served the purpose of God until He sent His Son Jesus Christ (see Gal. 3:15-29).

What's the bottom line in all of this? Jesus Christ has freed us from the technicalities of Sabbath law. He's the rest for our souls. The early church believed Christ had fulfilled the Sabbath law. And Scripture records they worshiped on Saturday, Sunday, and every day. The point isn't to make another day "the new Sabbath." The point is that Christ Himself is the Sabbath. The relationship He offers us is far better than ceremonies, dress codes, seasonal festivals, and even a specific Sabbath day! All of these are symbols that pointed to a Greater Reality. His name is Jesus Christ. If we are resting and rejoicing in His resurrection, we have fulfilled this Commandment.

What are the dangers in a legalistic keeping of the Sabbath?

How would you communicate the truth that Jesus has fulfilled the Sabbath law?

> Let us therefore no longer keep the Sabbath after the Jewish manner, and rejoice in days of idleness ... But let everyone of you keep the Sabbath after a spiritual manner, rejoicing in meditation on the law, ... And after the observance of the Sabbath, let every friend of Christ keep the Lord's Day as a festival, the resurrection-day, the queen and chief of all the days.[2]
>
> IGNATIUS (CIRCA 30-107)

GROUP STUDY

Warm Up

Christianity begins not with anything we do for God. It begins with receiving from, resting in, and remembering what God has done for us. But our continued obedience to God necessitates that we also find our continual rest in Him. Keeping the Fourth Commandment helps sustain us and our relationship with God as we pursue the world with the gospel. The message of our lives needs to match the message on our lips. The gospel we deliver should be an extension of what we are already living. The world is paying attention.

> In what ways is our mission affected by the unceasing drive to "do more" for God?

> How does the gospel give us the security and freedom to engage in God's mission out of delight, not duty?

Trust. Our trust God is shown by our obedience to God. If we trust Him, we obey Him knowing that He is responsible to meet our needs. If we don't, we do our own thing thinking we are in charge.

Delight. Our response to the Sabbath shows us that which we are excited about the most. It could be God and the gospel. It could be something else. Our actions reveal what we love in our hearts and value in our minds.

Rest. If we don't trust Christ, observing the Sabbath makes no sense. But if we do trust Jesus, then keeping this Commandment makes perfect sense. On "the Sabbath," we are to remember our relationship with God, delight in Him, and rest in His promise. Remember the promise from Jesus? We will find rest for our souls.

Discussion

The gospel tells the story of Jesus and the relationship He offers to us. But this story didn't begin with Jesus. It began at creation. When God declared the first Sabbath at creation, He rested in it. But then Adam fell into sin, so God got up from His Sabbath rest, so to speak, and started to work again. This time His work was not on creation but redemption. When Jesus rose from the dead, that work was completed. This is how Jesus' resurrection offers us a "new kind of Sabbath,"—a rest that comes from the work of redemption.

Use this time to share what God has revealed as you connect the dots and pursue the gospel. Some of the questions below are from your daily reading assignments. They will guide your small-group discussion.

1. Think about the rhythm of your own daily grind. How do you handle the hustle and bustle of your personal calendar? What drains you more than anything? What seems to fill you up?

2. What are some specific ways you have turned to work to define you and sustain you? How do you think Sabbath-keeping helps you refocus your mind's attention and heart's affection on God?

3. What are some ways people define their worth? What are the benefits of taking a day of rest each week to reflect on God and His goodness?

4. In your own words, how would you define rest? What's the difference between rest and relaxation (or leisure)? Can you rest while pursuing leisure?

5. What kind of "use and abuse" do you feel when you work? Is it self-imposed? What are the realistic options for you to make a change for the better?

6. How do you think keeping the Sabbath points to gospel? In what practical ways does the Sabbath direct you to rely upon God today?

7. In your own words, what does all of this mean for you today? How do you carve out time from your busy week to remember the redemptive work of God in your life?

Conclusion

The gospel is the most life-defining reality for all of us. It brings clarity to our lives. In Christ, we are fully loved and fully accepted by the only One whose opinion really matters. We don't have to base our self-worth on how successful we are, or how hard we work, or how much we produce.

The gospel is everything! It carries the full weight of God's love for us. It reveals the sustaining power of how God keeps us. But it embodies the expectation that God desires from us. Within the gospel itself is contained the power of God that brings salvation to everyone who believes (see Rom. 1:16). This salvation came first to the Jews who enjoyed a relationship with God through the law, and then to Gentiles who did not.

The gospel also reveals the righteousness of God. That is to say, the gospel story gives God the right to save anyone and everyone who will, by faith, believe in His Son Jesus Christ (see Rom. 1:16).

Let this gospel be your identity, your security, and your mission.

Spend some time praying this for you and for your group:

> "God, I want to find true rest in You. Help me find physical and spiritual rest in Jesus Christ—not some day in the week. I gladly surrender my heavy burdens to You. I humbly trust You, God, for my salvation. I commit my life to serving You as I carry the gospel to a broken world that needs You."

1. Timothy M. Pierce, *Enthroned on Our Praise: An Old Testament Theology of Worship* (Nashville: B&H Publishing, 2010), 71.
2. Ignatius, as quoted in J. B. Lightfoot and J.R. Harmer ed., *Apostolic Fathers* (Berkeley: Apocryphile Press, 2004), 181.
3. Craig L. Blomberg, "The Sabbath as Fulfilled in Christ," in *Perspectives on the Sabbath: 4 Views*, ed. Christopher John Donato (Nashville: B&H, 2011), 351.

Because Jesus fulfilled the Law, and thus fulfilled the Sabbath commands, He, not some day of the week, is what offers the believers rest. We obey the Sabbath Commandment of the Decalogue as we spiritually rest in Christ, letting Him bear our heavy burdens, trusting Him for salvation, and committing our lives to Him in service, then remaining faithful in lifelong loyalty to Him.[3]

CRAIG L. BLOMBERG

NOTES

SMALL-GROUP TIPS

Reading through this section and utilizing the suggested principles and practices will greatly enhance the group experience. First is to accept your limitations. You cannot transform a life. Your group must be devoted to the Bible, the Holy Spirit, and the power of Christian community. In doing so your group will have all the tools necessary to draw closer to God and to each other—and to experience heart transformation.

GENERAL TIPS:

- Prepare for each meeting by reviewing the material, praying for each group member, and asking the Holy Spirit to work through you as you point to Jesus each week.

- Make new attendees feel welcome.

- Think of ways to connect with group members away from group time. The amount of participation you have during your group meetings is directly related to the amount of time you connect with your group members away from the group meeting. Consider sending e-mails, texts, or social networking messages encouraging members in their personal devotion times prior to the session.

MATERIALS NEEDED:

- Bible

- Bible study book

- Pen/pencil

PROVIDE RESOURCES FOR GUESTS:

- An inexpensive way to make first-time guests feel welcome is to provide them a copy of your Bible study book. Estimate how many first-time guests you can expect during the course of your study, and secure that number of books. What about people who have not yet visited your group? You can encourage them to visit by providing a copy of the Bible study book.

SMALL-GROUP VALUES

Meeting together to study God's Word and experience life together is an exciting adventure. Here are values to consider for small-group experiences:

COMMUNITY: God is relational, so He created us to live in relationship with Him and one another. Authentic community involves sharing life together and connecting on many levels with others in our group.

INTERACTIVE BIBLE STUDY: God gave the Bible as our instruction manual for life. We need to deepen our understanding of God's Word. People learn and remember more as they wrestle with truth and learn from others. Bible discovery and group interaction will enhance spiritual growth.

EXPERIENTIAL GROWTH: Beyond solely reading, studying, and dissecting the Bible, being a disciple of Christ involves marrying knowledge and experience. We do this by taking questions to God, opening a dialogue with our hearts, and utilizing other ways to listen to God speak (other people, nature, circumstances, etc.). Experiential growth is always grounded in the Bible as God's primary revelation and our ultimate truth-source.

POWER OF GOD: Processes and strategies will be ineffective unless we invite and embrace the presence and power of God. In order to experience community and growth, Jesus needs to be the centerpiece of our group experiences, and the Holy Spirit must be at work.

REDEMPTIVE COMMUNITY: Healing best occurs within the context of community and relationships. It's vital to see ourselves through the eyes of others, share our stories, and ultimately find freedom from the secrets and lies that enslave our souls.

MISSION: God has invited us into a larger story with a great mission of setting captives free and healing the broken-hearted (see Isa. 61:1-2). However, we can only join in this mission to the degree that we've let Jesus bind up our wounds and set us free. Others will be attracted to an authentic, redemptive community.

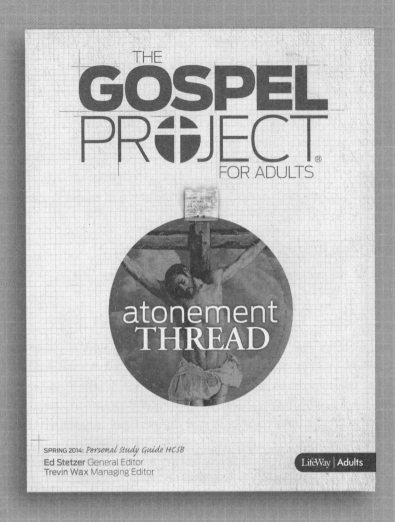

Continue the journey with The Gospel Project® ongoing studies...

Enjoying The Gospel Project?
If your group meets regularly, consider adopting
The Gospel Project as an ongoing Bible study series.

NEW STUDIES RELEASE EVERY THREE MONTHS.

Web: gospelproject.com
Twitter: @Gospel_Project
Facebook: TheGospelProject